Scallops
Sew
Easy

Marie
Seroskie

Love to
Quilt...

American Quilter's Society
P. O. Box 3290 • Paducah, KY 42002-3290
www.AmericanQuilter.com

D1476529

Located in Paducah, Kentucky, the American Quilter's Society (AQS) is dedicated to promoting the accomplishments of today's quilters. Through its publications and events, AQS strives to honor today's quiltmakers and their work and to inspire future creativity and innovation in quiltmaking.

EXECUTIVE EDITOR: NICOLE C. CHAMBERS
EDITOR: LINDA BAXTER LASCO
GRAPHIC DESIGN: ELAINE WILSON
COVER DESIGN: MICHAEL BUCKINGHAM
PHOTOGRAPHY: CHARLES R. LYNCH
HOW-TO PHOTOGRAPHY: MARIE SEROSKIE

Special thanks to J. Chad Wilson of Paducah's LowerTown Arts District for the use of his beautifully restored Vaughn-Blythe Mansion for our location photographs.

Library of Congress Cataloging-in-Publication Data

Morel-Seroskie, Marie
    Scallops sew easy: love to quilt / By Marie Seroskie.
       p. cm.
    Summary: "Patterns are provided for five sizes of easy-to-make scallop templates. Illustrated chapter detailing instructions on scalloped edges for quilting, home decor projects, and gift items. Fourteen illustrated projects with exceptional techniques"--Provided by publisher.
      ISBN 978-1-57432-935-3
      1. Quilting--Patterns. I. Title.

      TT835.S4534 2007
      746.46'041--dc22

               2007040265

Additional copies of this book may be ordered from the American Quilter's Society, PO Box 3290, Paducah, KY 42002-3290, or online at www.AmericanQuilter.com. For phone orders only 800-626-5420. For all other inquiries, call 270-898-7903.

Proudly printed and bound in the United States of America

Dedication

To my husband, Jim, who has supported and encouraged my life in the quilt world. Without him Katie Lane Quilts would only be the name of a street yet unexplored. To my parents, who provided private art lessons when they barely had two nickels to rub together.

Throughout all the years of owning Katie Lane Quilts, it is my husband who encourages and supports my quilt endeavors. Thank you my Jim.

To my brother Chuck Morel and my sister Therese Shannon. Their "you go girl" encouragement means a lot to me.

A special thanks to all the quilt students I've had the privilege to teach. It is you who taught me so very much – tips and techniques I would never have known about.

I am grateful to AQS who encouraged me to write this book after hearing a presentation on scallops, Nicole Chambers who massaged the text to make sense of it all, and to other AQS staff members who put the final touches to the finished text and pictures. I don't know all your names but you are thanked.

Table *of* Contents

Debunking
the
Scallop Myths

Scallops can make ordinary projects look special. They add style, personality, and even a little sassy chic, depending on how you use them. Often this simple and wonderful edging technique is passed over because it looks complicated. Nothing could be further from the truth if you know the tricks and techniques.

Contrary to what you may have heard, making scalloped edges is fun and easy. Had I been asked to scallop the edge of a quilt ten years ago, I would have been shaking in my shoes at the thought of having to know advanced calculus. Besides, salad bowls and dinner plates have their limitations as arc-shaped templates. Fortunately I have a husband who is a gifted engineer. By putting our heads together, we developed an easy technique for laying out a scalloped edge as well as the tools that make marking your project simple, accurate, and most importantly, convenient.

In this book, I hope to dispel some myths that may be keeping you from trying your own scalloped borders and inspire you to become a scallop aficionado instead.

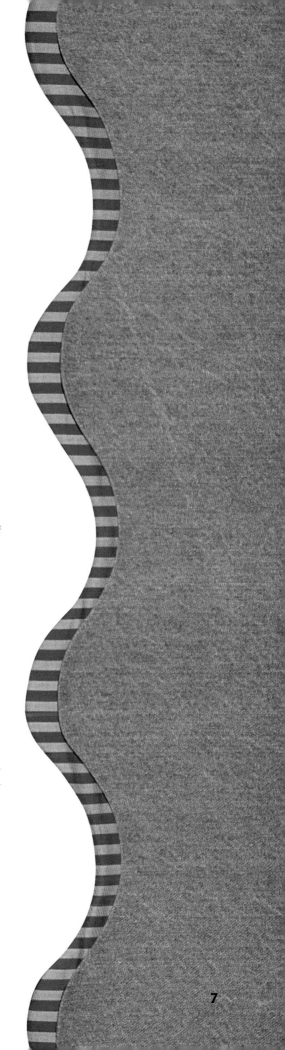

Figuring out the math is an absolute nightmare. Actually in this book I will show you the super easy steps of laying out your scallop border by the simple process of drawing your chosen scallops on a guideline. Yes, it really is that simple. The "math" disappears because you can make things fit by visually fudging a little here and a little there.

It requires at least a 42-piece set of china to design the perfect scalloped border. In this book you will find a set of five ready-to-use templates in the most popular scallop sizes. But even better yet, you will have a simple formula of how you can easily draft any custom-sized scallop template your heart desires.

You must use mitered borders anytime you scallop an edge. There is no hard and fast rule that borders must be mitered for the scalloped edge to look great. Wait until you see how easily you can scallop butted borders with fantastic results. Plus you'll learn how to make enough bias binding to bind a dozen quilts, as easy as pie!

Easy Techniques
for
Perfect Scallops

esign Considerations
Before we get started there are some things you will want to think about:

Does your project need the gentle arcs of serpentine scallops or the rounded curves of classic scallops?

Classic scallops are made from a succession of arcs all facing in the same direction. Serpentine scallops are more gentle curves formed by flipping the scallop 180° and thus need a little more space.

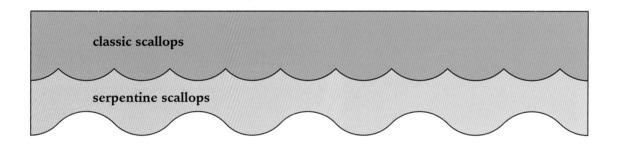

classic scallops

serpentine scallops

What size should the scallops be?

The best answer is to look at your project. A good rule of thumb is to choose a scallop size in proportion to your project. Using three 6" scallops on the long edge of your placemat may not give you the delicate look you have in mind – but if it is a look you love, there is nothing wrong with striking out on your own and following your personal vision.

Generally speaking, choose a scallop size that looks comfortable to your eye. You can easily preview your border design on freezer paper.

Don't be afraid of using a combination of two different scallops. A good rule of thumb is to use arcs that are 1" – 2" smaller or larger from each other. The idea is to blend them together rather than calling attention to their differences. On the other hand, sometimes you have to let your own creativity rule. If you have a great idea – try it.

You will also want to take the length of your border into consideration when deciding on a scallop size. You can easily decide what size scallop will give the best fit by dividing the border by the length of the scallop.

For example, if the edge of your quilt is 18" – nine 2" scallops or six 3" scallops will fit perfectly.

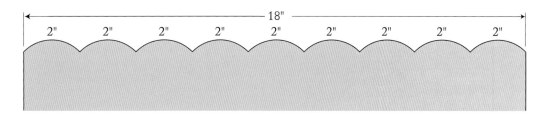

Length of project edge ÷ Length (size) of scallop = Number of scallops needed

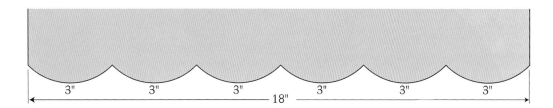

The big question is what to do when the border measures 18½" and you have that extra ½" to deal with? This is when you make the fudge factor work for you. By simply overlapping the arcs slightly or leaving small gaps in-between them, you can make the scallops look absolutely perfect. But more on the fudge factor later.

Let's get started ....

3 Easy Steps to Scalloping Success

1. DRAWING YOUR GUIDELINES

There are three types of projects:

- ❧ straight-line
- ❧ cornered
- ❧ round

Straight-line projects are things such as valances, pillowcases, skirts, and vests. As the name implies, you are simply scalloping a straight edge all the way across.

Cornered projects are things such as place mats, pillow shams, and quilts – items that are rectangular or square. For these kinds of projects you will need to scallop the corners.

Round projects make fun pillows, place mats and table toppers. They are easy, too – once you understand the art of fudging.

Gathering Your Tools

- ❧ Quilter's Template Plastic
- ❧ Freezer paper
- ❧ Sharpie® fine-tip permanent marker
- ❧ Pencil or ballpoint pen
- ❧ Clover® fine white marking pen
- ❧ Clover fine blue water-soluble marking pen
- ❧ General® white chalk marker
- ❧ Water-soluble thread*
- ❧ 50-or 60-weight sewing thread
- ❧ Open toe embroidery foot
- ❧ Pinking shears or pinking rotary blade
- ❧ Scallop rule (optional, but wonderful – see Resources, page 78)
- ❧ Chopstick

*For a specific technique

Scallops Sew EASY ❧ *Marie Seroskie*

No matter what type of project you are scalloping, you will start by first drawing guidelines that the scallops will rest on. When you are considering the placement of the guideline, you must make sure you have allowed enough fabric for the height of your scallops with at least ½" to spare. The longer scallops are, the more headroom they require.

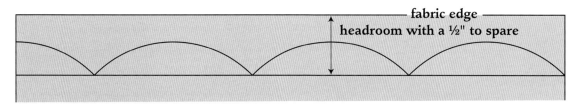

2. MAKE A SCALLOP TEMPLATE

On pages 27–28 You will find template patterns for five of the most popular scallop sizes (2", 3", 4", 5" and 6"). If you crave convenience, you can also use a commercially produced scallop rule that not only gives you a wide variety of scallop sizes but also a choice in the scallop's arc. Refer to the resources listed on page 78.

If your project requires a custom-sized scallop, you can easily draft your own template pattern in whatever size you wish by following the instructions found on page 26.

Begin by placing a piece of template plastic over the scallop pattern and hold it in place with tape. Using a fine point Sharpie permanent marker, trace the template outline onto the plastic. Be sure to include the center line and the 45° lines. Mark the length of the scallop as well as the headroom it requires.

Hint: *Scallop sizes tend to look similar so it's easy to mix them up when you are working with more than one template.*

Cut out your template with sharp scissors using long smooth strokes.

3. MARK THE SCALLOPS ON YOUR FABRIC BY TRACING THE TEMPLATE.

Mark the scallops on the **WRONG** side of the fabric if you are going to face the scalloped edge using another fabric. For scalloping quilts, you will want to draw your scallops on the **RIGHT** side of the quilted quilt.

For very light fabrics use a well-sharpened lead pencil. On dark fabrics or busy prints use a ballpoint pen. On ultra busy fabrics try a gel pen in red or another bright color that will make your lines easy to see. When you are marking very dark fabric, Clover fine white marking pen works very well on most fabrics.

You are now ready to scallop! The secret of perfect scalloped edges is two-fold. One – "The Approach" and two – how much of the "Fudge Factor" you will need to put into play.

The Approach
Straight-Edge Projects

The kind of project you are working on will define your approach to marking the scallops onto your guideline. For a single-edge project you have the choice of starting in the middle and working your way towards the outer edges. This works very well on items where it doesn't matter at what point the scallop ends on the outer edge.

Mark the center point of your guideline. Position the straight edge of your scallop template along the guideline, aligning the center mark of the template with the center of the guideline. Trace the scallop onto the fabric.

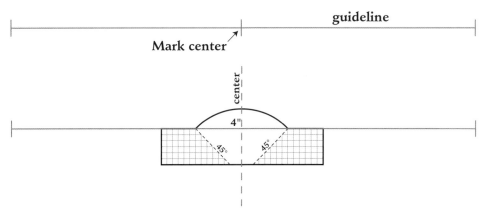

Slide the template to the left, next to the scallop you just drew and trace another scallop onto the fabric. Continue tracing scallops to the end of the guideline.

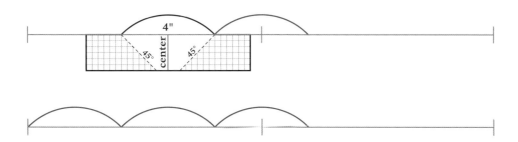

"The Rule" that must be obeyed ... (unless you have a totally cool design reason to ignore it) **... you MUST maintain symmetry** when placing your scallops. In other words, how you draw the scallops on the left, you should repeat on the right.

Making serpentine scalloped edges is equally simple. All the steps remain the same except that you will need to flip the template 180° after every scallop you trace to achieve the long sweeping curves.

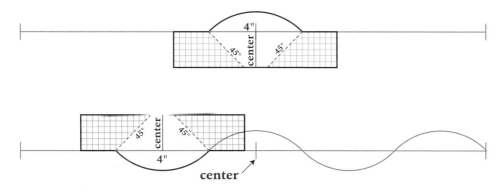

If your straight-edge project requires that the end scallops are completely formed, you will need to start at the outer edge of your guideline and work towards the center. If the center scallop is not a perfect fit, refer to The Art of Fudging on page 16 for some easy techniques to make it fit. Otherwise, start with the center scallop and work towards the outer edges.

Cornered Projects

The idea of scalloping corners makes most quilters want to run for the hills but it really is simple once you know how. Two complete scallops meeting form a scalloped corner. See, I told you it was easy.

To Miter or to Butt … that is the question. Fortunately it has an easy answer. First, you do not have to miter your corners for them to turn out beautifully scalloped. Second, if you love how a mitered corner looks, it is easily done … yes, really! Just refer to No Sweat Mitered Corners on page 25.

You are now ready to draw your scallops

Step 1: Draw your scallops in the corners first by positioning the scallop template so the starting point of the arc is meeting the corner of the guideline. Trace the first corner scallop (horizontal) onto the fabric. Refer to the left figure.

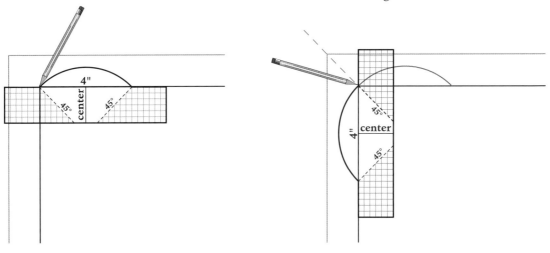

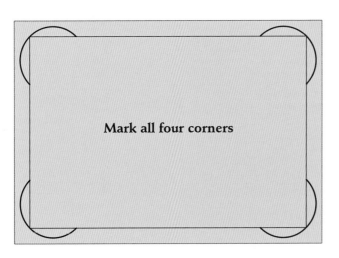

Mark all four corners

Step 2: Reposition the scallop template 90°, this time in a vertical position. Once again the starting point of the scallop must meet the corner of the guideline. Trace the second corner scallop onto the fabric. Refer to figure above. Repeat these steps for the remaining corners.

Step 3: Once the corner scallops have been defined, trace the remaining scallops working from the corners toward the center. If your scallops are not a perfect fit, refer to the techniques outlined in The Art of Fudging , page 16, for that perfect fit look.

Remember the rule that must be obeyed is that in most instances you should maintain symmetry when placing your scallops.

Cornered projects featuring serpentine scallops are handled the same way except that the template is flipped 180° with every scallop. Be sure to factor in that you will need to fit an odd number of scallops into the space if they are serpentine.

Use the formula below to determine how your scallops will fit within the designated space and how much fudging will be necessary:

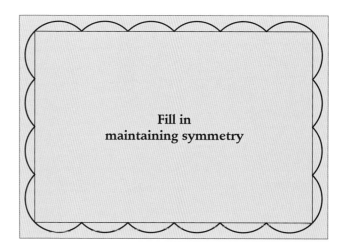

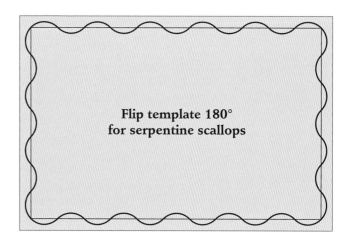

$$L \text{ (length of edge)} \div S \text{ (scallop size)} = N \text{ (number of scallops)}$$

The Art of Fudging

Take the art of fudging to heart and you are on your way to becoming a true scallop aficionado. As you work on various projects you will see that different situations call for different fixes. Choose the method or combination of methods that best suit your project and let's get scalloping.

Uniform Gap ~ when your space is too long for the size of scallop you are using: In instances where you have a fraction of an inch left over, consume the extra fraction by spreading the scallops ever so slightly. Leave ¹⁄₁₆" to ⅛" in between your scallops. The gaps won't show because you will take one to three more stitches as you sew the scalloped seam. For example, if your edge measures 30½", ignore the ½" and use a scallop size that will fit into a 30" space.

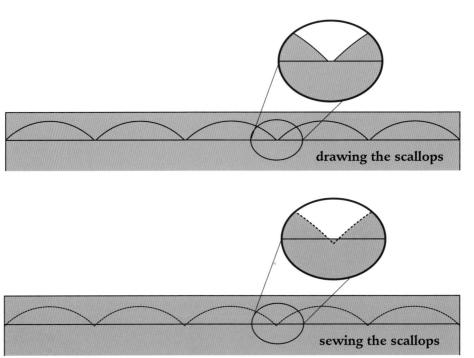

drawing the scallops

sewing the scallops

Overlap Technique ~ when your space is too short for the size scallop you are using: In instances where you have an edge that is a fraction of an inch too short, slightly overlap the scallops. For example if your edge measures 29½", round the number up to 30" and use a scallop size that will fit into that space. Overlap the scallops ever so slightly as you mark them on the guideline.

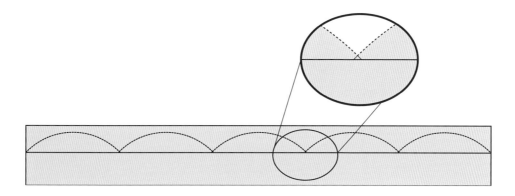

CENTER SCALLOP OVERLAP

This is a great multipurpose fudging technique for many different projects. Working from the corners (or outer edges) towards the center, leave a gap in the middle that is slightly smaller or larger than the scallop you are using.

In cases when the center space is smaller ~ Overlap the center scallop onto the arcs on each side. The middle arc can be a different size since it sits on top of the adjacent scallops. Use a subtle approach by choosing a scallop size that is close to that of the adjacent ones and keep the top of the scallop even with the others.

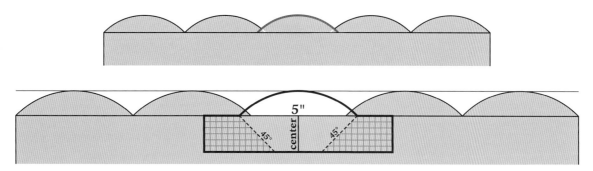

In cases when the space is slightly larger ~ Use a larger scallop and place it so the top of that center scallop is at the same height as the others. This will make it blend in even though it is a different size.

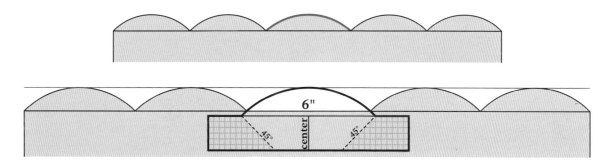

Combining 2 different sizes of scallops ~ Sometimes you can get the best fit and look by combining several scallop sizes. In those instances you can leave a gap large enough to fit 2 or 3 smaller or larger scallops in that space. Just remember you need to keep them centered for the border to look balanced.

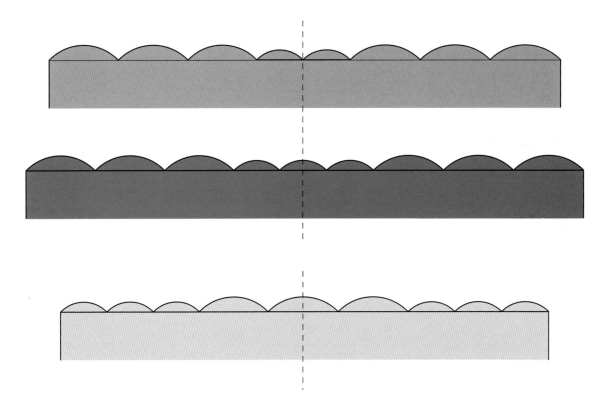

These fudging techniques work just as well and in the same way when you are making serpentine scallops. Just be sure to take into consideration that with corner-edged projects you will need an odd number of scallops to make the serpentine fit.

WHAT IF ONE SIDE OF YOUR QUILT IS TOO LONG AND THE OTHER SIDE IS TOO SHORT?

Let's say that the quilt you want to scallop measures 60½" on the short sides and 69½" on the long sides. Relax, it's ok to use more than one fudging technique in a single project.

Based on some easy math (length of edge divided by scallop size), you know that 12 five-inch scallops will fit nicely along the short edge. But what about that pesky ½" that's left over? Treat that side of the quilt as though it measures 60", and use the Uniform Gap fudging technique by leaving a little bit of space in between each scallop.

What do you do about the other sides of the quilt that are ½" too short? In this instance you will use the Uniform Overlap technique and overlap neighboring scallops ever so slightly. Yes, a perfectly scalloped quilt really is that easy. Just remember to do your corners first!

Previewing Your Scalloped Edge with Freezer Paper

Previewing how your scallops will look is always a good idea, plus in many instances you can use a freezer-paper mock-up as a template. You can make a multitude of scalloped place mats quickly by simply pressing the freezer-paper template onto fabric and tracing. Presto, your placemats are ready to sew.

To do a mock-up of small projects, draw your guideline to size, be it a straight line, circle, square, or rectangle. On a large project such as a quilt, you can mock up ¼ of the quilt (from center to corner). That way you can see how your scallops will look and not have unwieldy amounts of freezer paper to work with.

Easy Finishing Techniques

TURNED EDGE OR FACED SCALLOPS

Sew 2 layers of fabrics together, and then turn them right side out to create many beautiful scalloped effects. This technique requires no binding and suits many different kinds of projects.

It's a good rule of thumb to press fabric layers right sides together with an iron. Projects that require batting will need to have the batting added at the bottom of these 2 layers. In other words, start with the batting then add fabric #1 (right side up) and fabric #2 (wrong side up). The fabric with the scallop markings should be facing you.

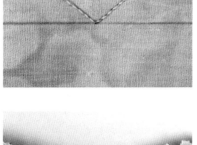

Pin layers together using 2 pins per scallop to make sure nothing will shift.

Use a fine 50- or 60- weight cotton thread in your machine and in the bobbin. The thinner thread will make turning and pressing the seams much easier. Shorten the stitch length to 12 – 14 stitches per inch (approximately 1.5 on most sewing machines).

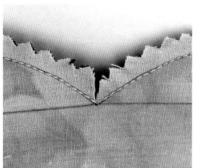

Using an open toe embroidery foot, stitch directly on the drawn scallop lines.

Trim scallops so the seam allowance is a little less than ¼" using pinking shears or a pinking rotary-cutting blade. Clip the inside V where the scallops meet with very sharp pointed scissors. Be careful not to clip into the seam itself.

Shortcut

Projects that will need to be completely turned inside out, such as placemats, can be sewn completely around. Instead of leaving an opening for turning and then stitching it closed, cut a slit through one layer and use that opening to turn the fabrics right side out. Later you can cover the slit with an appliqué to hide the hole.

Turn fabrics right side out making sure each scallop is smoothly poked out. A great turning tool is a chopstick.

Nice girls do spit … and roll, that is. Before pressing the scalloped edge with an iron, give your thumb and index finger a little tongue-lashing. This will give you the traction you need to roll the stitched scallop edges so they sit one on top of another with neither one peeking through to the other side. Press with a hot iron.

BINDING

Scallops must be bound with bias binding. For best results use binding between 2" – 2¼" wide.

Begin by determining how much binding you will need. A good rule of thumb to determine the length of binding you will need for a scalloped edge is to add 1" for each scallop to the measurement of the quilt's edge.

For example, if the quilt top measures 50" x 60" and you have 10 scallops on both of the 50" sides and 12 scallops on both of the 60" sides, you would figure the binding length needed as follows:

50" (quilt) + 10" (1" for 10 scallops) = 60"
60" x 2 (for top/bottom of quilt) = 120"

60" (quilt) + 12" (1" for 12 scallops) = 72"
72" x 2 (for each side of the quilt) = 144"

120" + 144" = 264" + 12" (for insurance) = 276"
276" of binding needed for this quilt.

MAKING MOUNTAINS OF BIAS BINDING IN A FLASH

You can use any size square to make binding using this technique. Here is the formula to tell you how much binding you will get from any square:

Width x Length of the square = Square inches

Example: 17" (width) x 17" (length) = 289" (square inches of square)

Square inches ÷ width of binding = length of bias strip

Example: 289" ÷ 2" (width of binding) = 144.5"

A 17" square will yield 144.5" of binding.

Bias Binding

Size of Square in inches	2" Binding in inches	2¼" Binding in inches
17	144	128
18	162	144
20	200	177
22	242	215
24	288	256
26	338	300
28	392	348
30	450	400
34	578	513
36	648	576
38	722	641
40	800	711

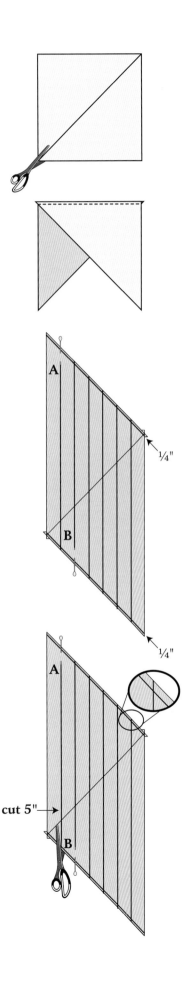

To make your binding tube, cut the square in half on the diagonal with the right side facing up. Take the bottom triangle, flip it over, top to bottom, and place it right side to right side on top of the other triangle. Stitch a ¼" seam.

Press the seam allowance open. Using a ruler, mark ¼" along each non-bias edge of the fabric.

Draw the cutting lines the width of the bias binding you are making (2" or 2¼"). Notice how these lines intersect the ¼" seam line previously drawn. This X will save you time when matching those two edges. Cut 5" on the first drawn line.

Note the placement of the pin on side A and side B. With right sides together, pin A and B sides matching the two pins at the X points. Sew a ¼" seam along this edge. The offset creates a spiral (instead of a donut) and when you cut on the pencil line, your strip will be continuous.

With the tip of the iron press the seam open. Continue cutting the fabric from the spot you had originally started cutting.

BINDING YOUR PROJECT

With wrong sides together, press binding in half lengthwise.

Mark your scallop border on the front of the quilt after it has been quilted. **DO NOT cut out the scalloped edge.** You must apply the binding to the quilt before trimming the edges. Generally, you will get a better result if you don't use pins.

Begin applying the binding at a corner. Leaving a tail of 4" to 5", butt the raw edge of the binding to the drawn scallop line and stitch ¼" from the raw edge of the binding.

When you come to an inside V, position the machine needle down, lift the presser foot and pivot the fabric. When you pivot the fabric, the binding tends to scrunch and get in the way. Be sure to push the binding up and away from the needle and seam line. Lower the presser foot, and resume stitching.

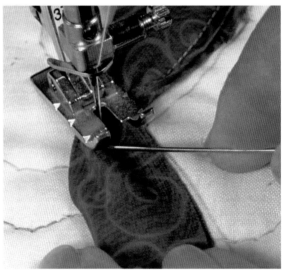

Stitch all the way around the quilt until you are about 5" from the tail you left at the beginning.

To mark the place where the ends of the binding strip will need to be joined, overlap the ends, placing the starting end on top. Mark the location with a diagonal line. Add ½" of extra length to that mark for seam allowance and draw a 45° cutting line. Open folded binding strip and cut along this line. Sew ends of binding together using a diagonal seam.

Fingerpress seam open and then refold binding again. Pin loose binding in place and sew to the quilt.

Trim the backing and batting on the drawn scallop line along the raw edges of the binding.

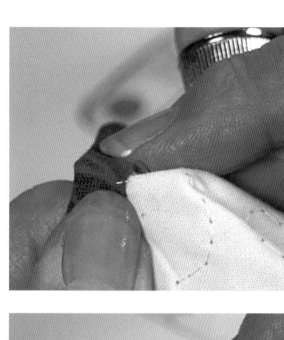

Fold binding over the raw edge to the back of the quilt. Your binding will look best if it just barely covers the stitched seam allowance as you hand sew it to the back.

When you come to the Vs between the scallops, snip the seam allowance of the quilt but NOT the binding.

Stretch the scallops apart as you stitch down into the V. Make sure the binding remains straight, and is not twisting.

Take two small extra stitches in the point of the V. Keep shaping the fabric to the curves of the scallops as you stitch the binding in place.

To make your scallops lie flat in places where you may have pulled the binding too tightly, hold a steam iron over the scallops without touching the quilt. Let some heat and moisture penetrate the bound edge, then gently finger press the scallops flat.

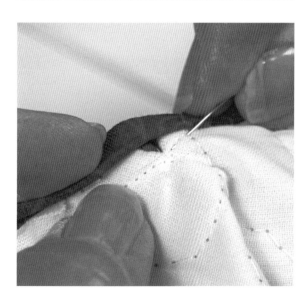

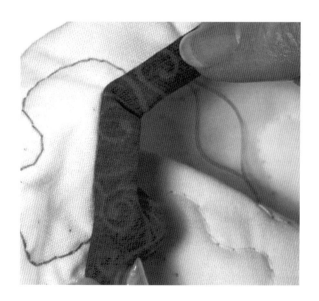

Scallops Sew EASY ❧ *Marie Seroskie*

ℳo Sweat Mitered Corners

Using diagonal seams, piece borders together so they measure the length (or width) of the quilt plus twice the width of the border and an additional 4 inches. For example, if your border is 5" wide and your quilt is 60" long, you will want your border strip to measure 74" (60 + 5 + 5 + 4 = 74).

Fold the border in half and mark the center with a pin. With right sides together and raw edges even, match the center of the border strip to the center of the quilt and pin the border and quilt together.

Starting and ending ¼" short of the quilt's edge, sew the border to quilt. Be sure to lock your beginning and ending stitches.

Sew borders onto the remaining three sides using the same technique. Press seams toward the outer edge.

Turn the quilt so the wrong side is facing you and begin by laying a corner flat with ends of border strips extended. Fold the top border strip at a 45° angle and press. On the right side, place the folded border on top and secure with a piece of masking tape. Open the fold and sew in the crease you have just pressed in. Remove tape and cut the seam allowance to measure ¼". Press the seam open. Miter the remaining 3 corners following this technique.

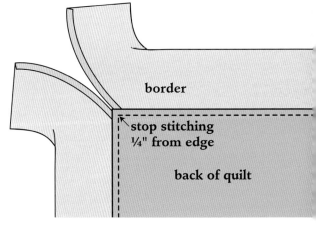

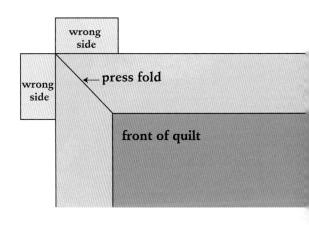

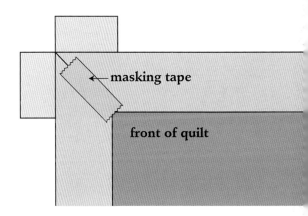

Drafting
your own
Custom Scallop Templates

You can make your own scallop templates any size you wish. Simply follow these easy steps:

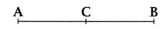

1. Draw a horizontal line and mark two end points of the scallop you want to make (A and B). Label the halfway point as C. The distance between A and B is the length of the scallop.

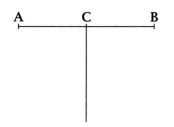

2. Draw a vertical line from the center point C forming a long T.

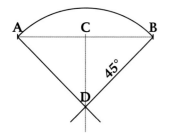

3. Use a triangle rule to draw a 45° line from points A and B towards the center, line C. Label the point where they intersect as D.

4. Use a compass or string and pencil to draw an arc through A and B using point D as the center of the curve.

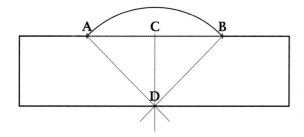

5. Add side "wings" to the scallop to help with alignment. Trace onto Quilter's Template Plastic with a fine tip marker and you are ready to rock 'n roll.

Scallops Sew EASY ✧ *Marie Seroskie*

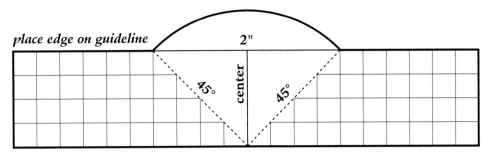

place edge on guideline

2"

45° center 45°

2" arc template pattern

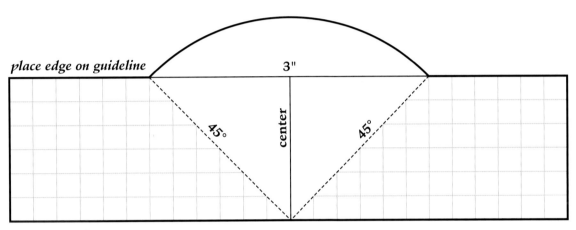

place edge on guideline

3"

45° center 45°

3" arc template pattern

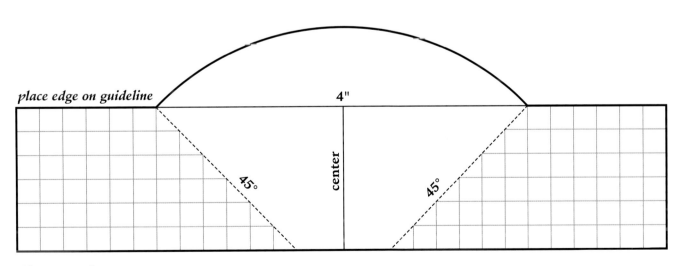

place edge on guideline

4"

45° center 45°

4" arc template pattern

Scallop Templates

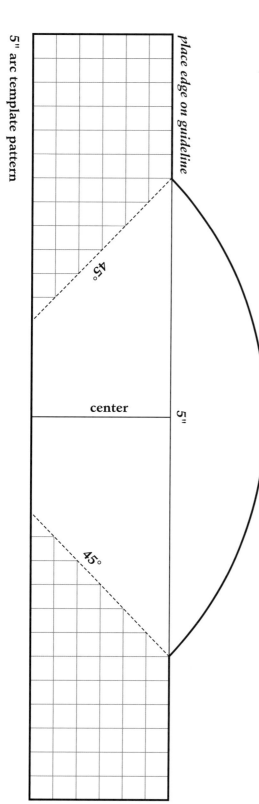

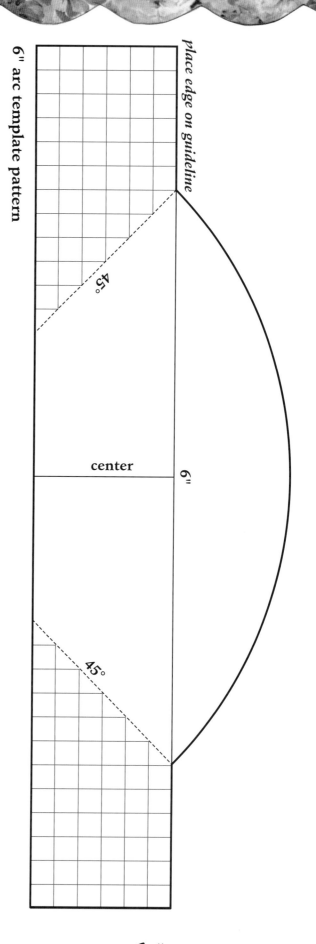

Scallop Templates

Projects

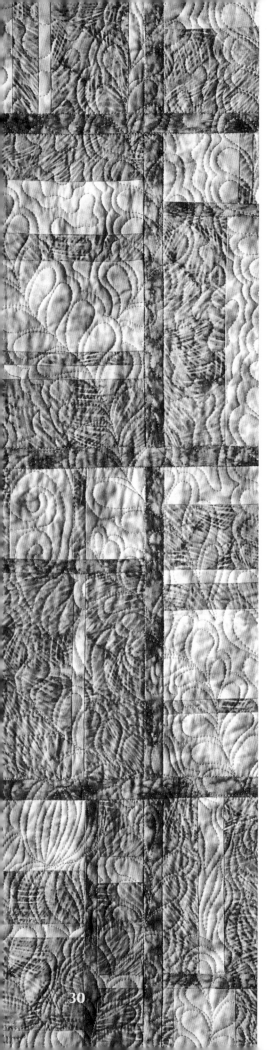

Paris Rendezvous
56" x 68½"

Fabric Requirements

Three different values of batik, or tone-on-tone fabrics,
all the same color

Light (blocks and inner border)	3 yards
Medium (blocks)	3½ yards
Dark (sashing and scalloped border)	2 yards
Backing	4½ yards
Batting	64" x 78"

Supplies

5" scallop template
Water-soluble thread
Freezer paper

Cutting Instructions (Fabric must be at least 42" wide)

Blocks & Sashing

Light fabric

4 strips	4" wide	Cut into (10) 14" sections
4 strips	3½" wide	Cut into (10) 14" sections
4 strips	3" wide	Cut into (10) 14" sections
4 strips	2½" wide	Cut into (10) 14" sections
4 strips	2" wide	Cut into (10) 14" sections
4 strips	1½" wide	Cut into (10) 14" sections
4 strips	1" wide	Cut into (10) 14" sections

Medium fabric

4 strips	4" wide	Cut into (10) 14" sections
4 strips	3½" wide	Cut into (10) 14" sections
4 strips	3" wide	Cut into (10) 14" sections
4 strips	2½" wide	Cut into (10) 14" sections
4 strips	2" wide	Cut into (10) 14" sections
4 strips	1½" wide	Cut into (10) 14" sections
4 strips	1" wide	Cut into (10) 14" sections

Dark fabric
7 strips	1" wide	Cut into (20) 14" sections
5 strips	1½" wide	Cut into (15) 12½" sections
6 strips	1½" wide	joined with a bias seam and cut into (4) 51½" strips

Inner border
| 7 strips | 4" wide | joined with a bias seam |

Scalloped Border
| 7 strips | 4" wide | joined with a bias seam |

Blocks

Using a ¼" seam allowance, sew seven 14" strips together using one strip of each width for each block. Alternate the light and medium fabrics. Be sure to arrange strips for each strip set randomly but do not position the 1" or 1½" strip on the ends of the strip-sets. Press seams in one direction.

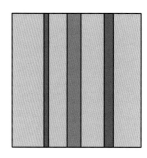

For the sake of clarity strips are shown in different colors.

Lay two blocks together, right sides up. With the lines on your rotary ruler aligned with the seam lines on the blocks, cut the blocks into 2 randomly sized segments.* Trade two of the same size segments between the two blocks. Feel free to flip one of the segments around for a more interesting arrangement of the strips. Join two segments by sewing a 1" x 14" strip of the dark fabric between them. Trim each block to measure 12½". Repeat with the remaining 18 blocks.

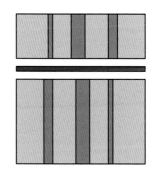

***Cutting Hint:** Cut one set of blocks in half, another set in thirds, and others according to whim.*

Arrange the blocks into 5 rows with 4 blocks in each row. Alternate the horizontal and vertical orientation of the strips in the blocks to create a pleasing effect. Lay a 1½" x 12½" sashing strip between the four blocks in each row. Sew the blocks and sashing strips into rows. Join the rows with a 51½" sashing strip between them (see page 32). Press.

Paris Rendezvous

Measure the length of the quilt through the center and cut two 4" inner border strips to that measurement. Stitch to the sides of the quilt. Press the seam allowance toward the outer edge. Measure the width of the quilt through the center and cut two 4" inner border strips to that measurement. Stitch to top and bottom of the quilt.

Cut the backing fabric into two panels, trimming off the selvage. Join the two panels and press the seams open.

Layer the quilt top, batting, and backing and quilt as desired.

Paris Rendezvous

Scalloped Border

Measure the length of the quilt top and cut a 5" wide piece of freezer paper that length. Repeat for the width of the quilt. Draw two guidelines the length of the freezer paper 2" apart. Draw 5" scallops on each guideline as illustrated.

For the outer scallops, start at the center, aligning the center point of the scallop template with the center point of the freezer paper and draw a line of 5" scallops along the lower guideline.

For inner scallops, start at the center, aligning the edge of the 5" scallop template with the center of the freezer paper and draw a line of 5" scallops along the upper guideline. Cut out the patterns along the drawn lines of scallops.

Measure the length of the quilt and add ½" to that measurement. Cut two 4" strips to that length from the dark fabric. Draw a guideline on the wrong side of each strip 1½" from the edge. Press the freezer-paper pattern to the wrong side of the border strip, aligning the bottom guideline of the pattern with the guideline on the fabric. Trace all the scallops onto the fabric. Repeat these steps for the width measurement of the quilt.

The scalloped border is turned under and applied to the edges of the quilt in the same way that the accent strip on the decorator towel is done. Follow the Sewing the Border instructions on pages 55–56 for the super easy technique to turn under the top edge of the scallops by sewing with water-soluble thread.

With wrong sides together, sew the two side scalloped borders to the quilt, trim seam allowance with pinking shears, clip Vs and turn to the right side. Topstitch in place. Repeat for the top and bottom of the quilt. Be sure to continue the scallops to the edge. After turning the top and bottom borders to the right side, trim and tuck under the seam allowances at the ends before topstitching, and secure them with the topstitching.

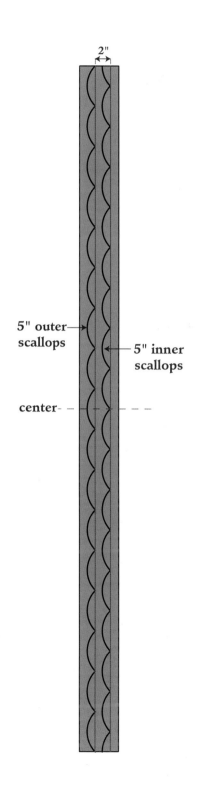

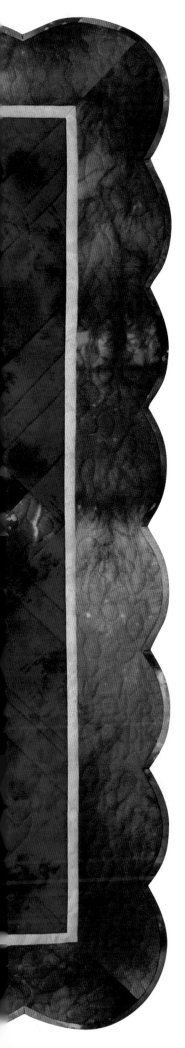

Calla Lily
44" x 44"

Fabric Requirements

Multicolored hand-dyed print –
be sure this fabric has many different color variations
(background, border, binding)   3¾ yards

Blue (corner triangles)	⅝ yard
Yellow (inner border, lilies)	¼ yard
3 Medium Greens (leaves)	3 fat quarters
Light Green (stems)	fat quarter
White-on-white (lilies)	¾ yard
Backing	1½ yard
Batting	50" x 50" square

Supplies

5" scallop template
Fabric crayons

Cutting Instructions

Multicolored hand-dyed print

Center blocks

2 strips	4" wide	Cut into (4) 14" sections
2 strips	3½" wide	Cut into (4) 14" sections
2 strips	3" wide	Cut into (4) 14" sections
2 strips	2½" wide	Cut into (4) 14" sections
2 strips	2" wide	Cut into (4) 14" sections
2 strips	1½" wide	Cut into (4) 14" sections
2 strips	1" wide	Cut into (8) 14" sections

Border

4 strips	4½" wide

Corner triangles

2	17⅞" squares	Cut in half diagonally once

Inner border

4 strips	1½"

Calla Lily

For the sake of clarity strips are shown in different colors.

Blocks (Multicolored hand-dyed print)

Using a ¼" seam allowance, sew seven 14" strips together using one of each width for each block. Press seams open. Be sure to arrange strips for each strip-set randomly but do not position the 1" and 1½" strips on the ends. Trim the top and bottom of the blocks so edges are even.

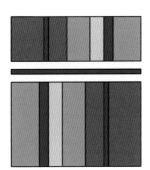

Cut each block into 2 random segments. For example, cut one block in half, one in a third and so on. Flip one cut segment around so the strips and color are in the opposite order. Join the two segments together by sewing a 1" x 14" strip between these two segments. Trim each block to measure 12½".

Arrange the blocks to create a pleasing effect and sew them together. Press seams open.

Mark the center of the wide edge of each corner triangle. Line up the triangle center and the center of the pieced 4-block unit. Sew the triangle to the unit and press the seam allowance toward the triangle. Repeat on the remaining 3 sides.

Scallops Sew EASY *Marie Seroskie*

Measure the quilt through the center and cut two 1½" inner border strips to that measurement. Stitch to sides of the quilt. Press the seam allowance toward the outer edge. Repeat these steps and attach inner borders to the top and bottom of the quilt.

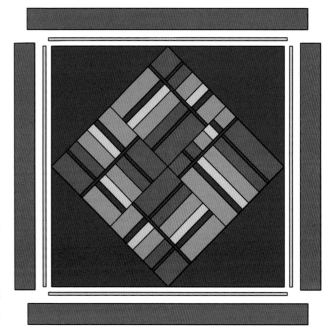

Attach the outer border to your quilt. Press seam allowances toward the outer edge. As an alternative, follow the instructions for the No Sweat Mitered Corners on page 25.

Apply calla lilies to the center of your quilt using your favorite appliqué method. Appliqué templates are found on pages 38–40.

Note: The lily templates are reversed for your convenience.

Scalloping the Edge

Measure 2¾" from the inner border seam line and draw a guideline on the right side of the quilt. Using the 5" scallop template, mark the scallops on the outer border following the instructions on pages 14–15.

Layer the quilt top, batting, and backing and quilt as desired. Bind the scalloped edge following the instructions found on pages 23–24.

Calla Lily
FLOWER 1

Note: The calla lily templates are reversed for your convenience.

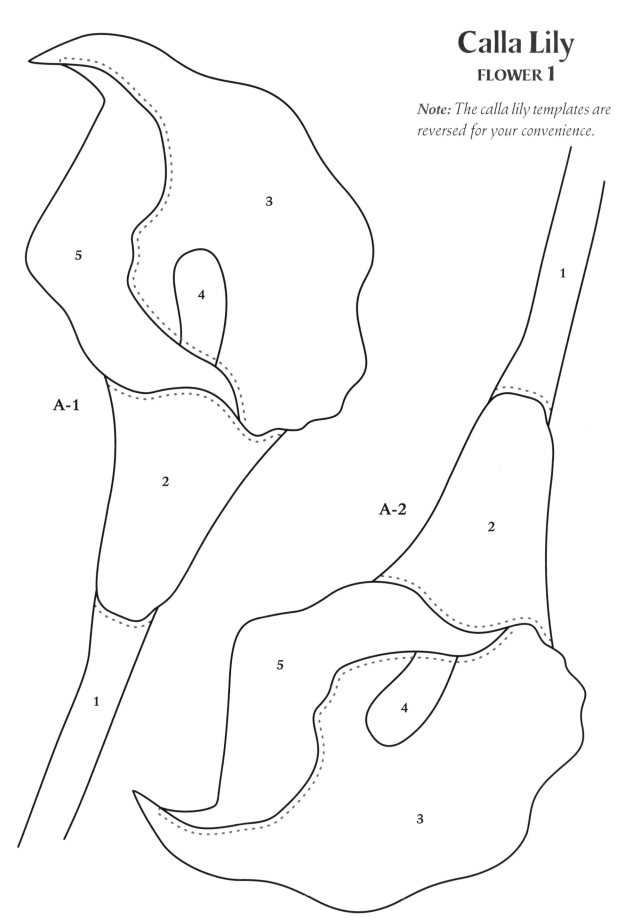

A-1

A-2

3

5

4

2

1

2

5

4

1

3

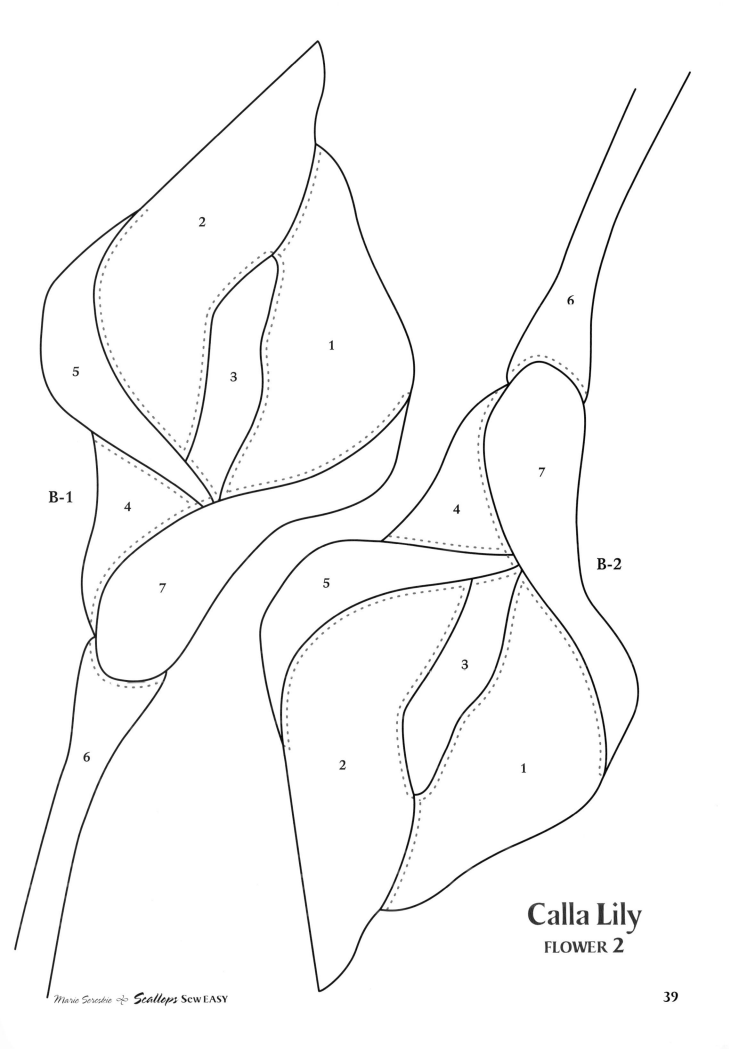

B-1

B-2

Calla Lily
FLOWER **2**

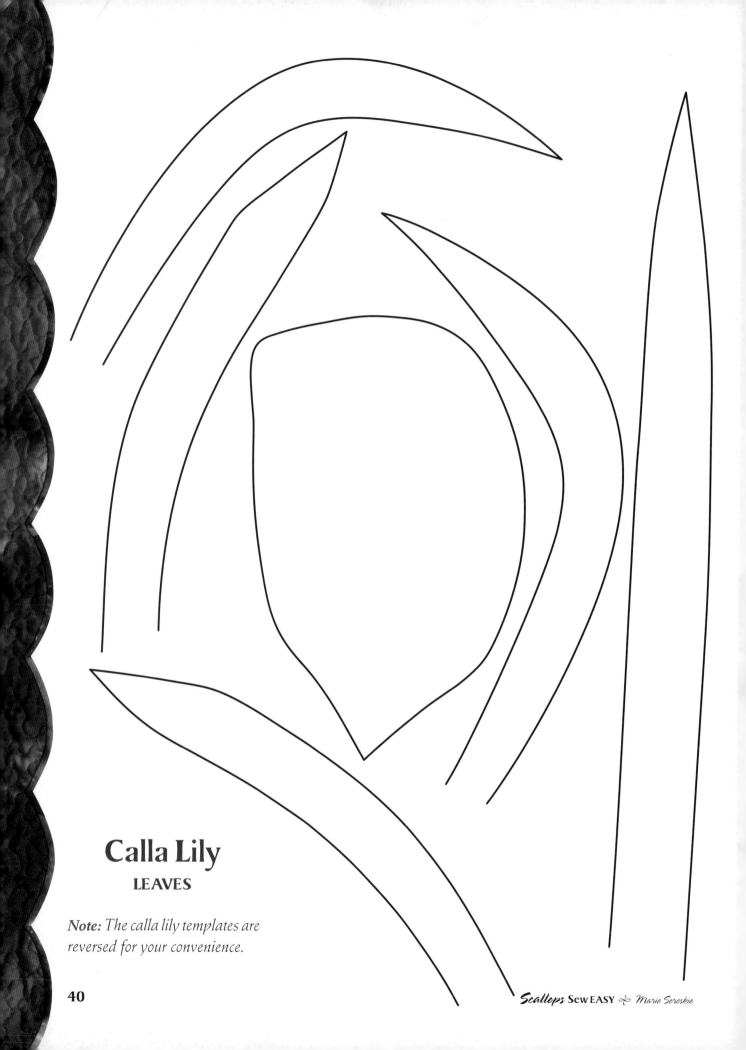

Calla Lily

LEAVES

Note: The calla lily templates are reversed for your convenience.

Dogwood Table Runner
17" x 40"

Fabric Requirements:

Medium tan	¼ yard
Off-white	1⅜ yards
Pink (flowers/scallops)	½ yard
Green (leaves)	¼ yard
Dark brown (branches)	fat quarter
Backing	⅝ yard
Batting (thin)	⅝ yard
Fusible web	1 yard

Nonstick pressing sheet
2", 3", and 5" scallop templates

Cutting Instructions:
Medium Tan

1 strip	4½" wide	Cut into (4) 4⅞" squares
1 strip	9⅜" wide	Cut into (4) 9⅜" squares cut in half diagonally once
1 strip	2⅞" wide	Cut into (8) 2⅞" squares
1 strip	3½" wide	Cut into (2) 3½" x 17½" rectangles

Off-white

1 strip	6⅞" wide	Cut into (4) 6⅞" squares cut in half diagonally once
1 strip	2⅞" wide	Cut into (12) 2⅞" squares

Dogwood Table Runner

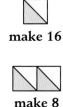

make 16

make 8

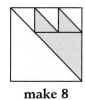

make 8

make 8

make 2

Sewing Instructions

Place 8 tan and off-white 2⅞" squares right sides together. Cut them in half diagonally. Sew the triangles together on the wide edge. Press the seam towards the darker fabric and trim off dog ears.

Sew 2 half-square triangles together as illustrated.

Cut the remaining off-white 2⅞" squares in half diagonally and sew onto the half-square triangle units as illustrated.

Then add a tan (4⅞") triangle. Press the seam toward the tan triangle.

Sew an off-white (6⅞") triangle onto this unit and press the seam towards the large triangle.

Sew 4 units together to make a block as illustrated. Press seams in the directions the arrows indicate.

Undo several stitches in the seam allowance at the center of the block so block lays flat.

Sew the tan fabric (9⅜") triangles onto the 4 corners of each block as illustrated. Press the seam toward the outer edge as you work. Your finished blocks should measure 17½".

Sew the blocks together. Then add a 3½" x 17½" rectangle onto each end.

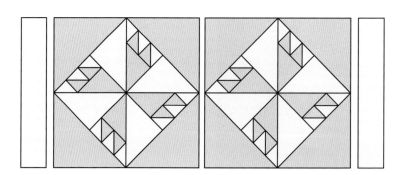

Scallops SEW EASY ℒ *Marie Seroskie*

SCALLOPED INSET

On the wrong side of a 1¼" x 35" strip, draw a guideline ¾" up from the outer edge. Mark the center of the strip and then draw 2 vertical lines ½" from both ends.

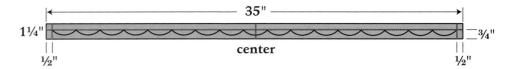

Using the 2" scallop template and starting at the center, draw scallops from the center out to ½" from each end. There should be a total of 17 scallops.

With right sides together, pin the marked strip and the unmarked strip together. Using a small stitch length of 12 – 14 stitches per inch, stitch the marked scallops and the vertical lines on each end.

Trim the seam allowance to measure a scant ¼" using pinking shears. Clip Vs where the two scallops meet, taking care not to cut the seam. Turn right side out and press.

With raw edges even, pin the scallop insets to the right sides of the table runner. The finished scallops should be facing towards the center of the table runner. Stitch ⅛" from the outer edge to hold in place until the binding has been applied.

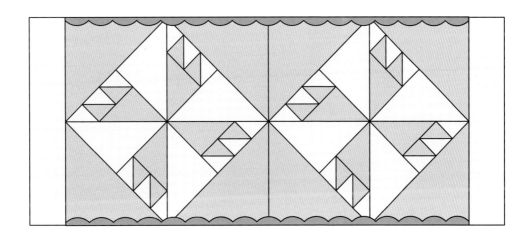

Dogwood Table Runner

Apply dogwood blossoms to the table runner using your favorite appliqué method. Appliqué templates are found on page 47.

Note: The dogwood templates are reversed for your convenience.

SCALLOPING TABLE RUNNER ENDS

Find the center of both ends of the table runner and mark with a pin. Draw a guideline 2" from the outer edge on both ends of the table runner.

On the wrong side of the table runner top, draw a 5" scallop in the center and then two 3" scallops on each side of it. Repeat on the other side. Layer the table runner top, batting, and backing together and quilt as desired. Bind scalloped and straight edges following the instructions found on pages 23–24.

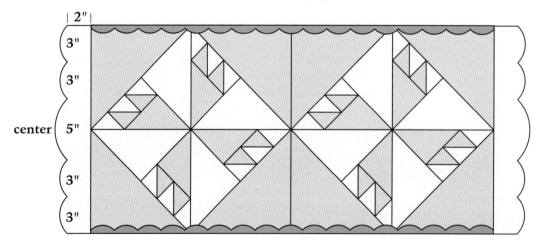

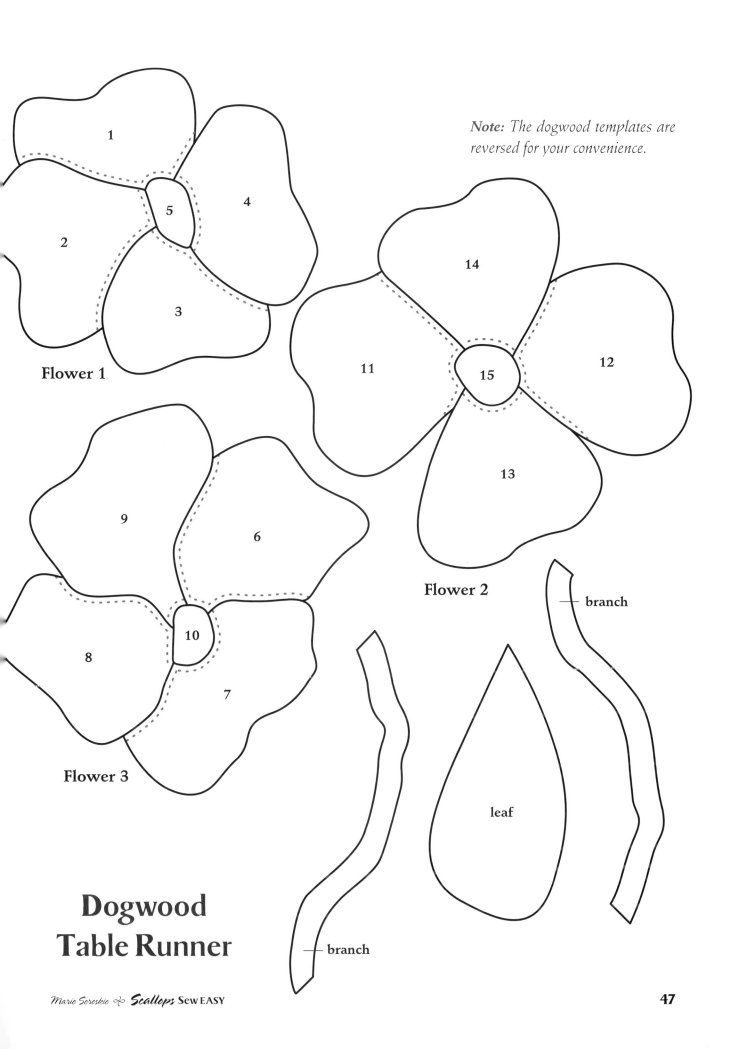

Note: The dogwood templates are reversed for your convenience.

Flower 1

Flower 2

Flower 3

branch

leaf

branch

Dogwood Table Runner

Scalloped Table Runner
13" x 37"

Supplies:
  ½ yard floral print
  ½ yard tone-on-tone print
  Freezer paper
  3" scallop template

Cut freezer paper 16" x 40" for the table runner pattern.

Draw a 12" x 36" rectangle; these are your guidelines.

Starting at the corners, draw 3" scallops along all four sides of the rectangle. Cut out the pattern.

MAKING THE TABLE RUNNER
Make the table runner referring to the Turned Edge or Faced Scallops instructions on pages 20–21.

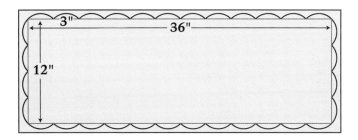

Note: Before sewing the table runner together, stitch a 2" line of stay-stitching on one corner of the scallop pencil line. This line of stitching marks the opening you will leave for turning the table runner right side out. It will also help create a smooth curve when you press the turned hem.

After trimming the seam allowance and clipping the Vs between the scallops, turn fabrics right side out making sure each scallop is poked out. Press the table runner flat. Press the seam allowance of the opening toward the inside of the table runner. Use the stay-stitching at the corner opening to help press a smooth curve.

Slip stitch the opening closed.

Tip: A great inexpensive turning tool is a chopstick.

Mochaccino • Cafe Con
Espresso • Americano • Mocha
Macchiato • Java • Cafe au
Cafe Misto • Breve • Granita
Mochaccino • Cafe Con
Cappuccino • Latte • Coffee
Espresso • Americano • Mocha
Au Lait • Macchiato • Java • Cafe
Cafe Misto • Breve • Granita
Con Leche • Mochaccino • Cafe Con
Coffee • Cappuccino • Latte • Coffee
Mocha • Espresso • Americano • Mocha
Cafe Au Lait • Macchiato • Java • Cafe au
Granita • Cafe Misto • Breve • Granita

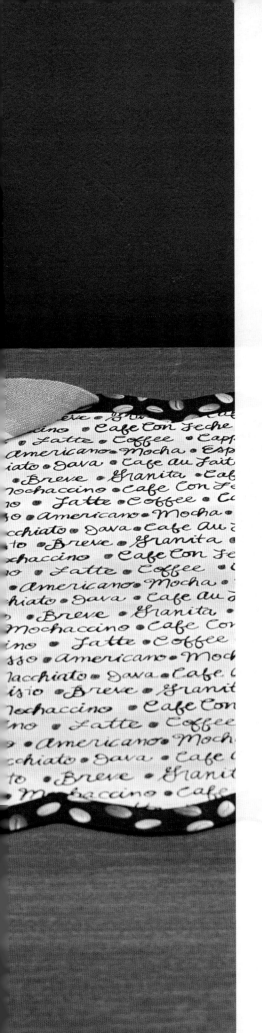

Double Scalloped Placemat

Supplies:
- ½ yard coffee bean print
- ½ yard black backing
- ½ yard scalloped center inset print
- ½ yard throwaway muslin
- Water-soluble thread
- Freezer paper
- 3" scallop template
- 4" scallop template

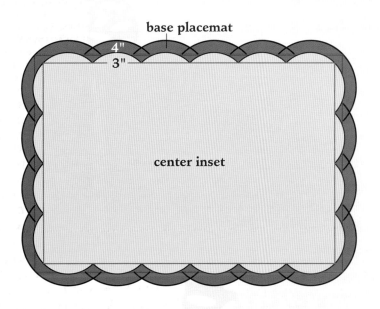

base placemat

4"

3"

center inset

Making the Master Pattern

Cut freezer paper 16" x 22" for the master pattern. Draw a 14" x 20" rectangle; these are your guidelines for the base placemat scallops.

Draw a 12" x 18" rectangle within the 14" x 20" rectangle; these are your guidelines for the placemat inset scallops.

Beginning with the placemat inset corners, draw 3" scallops along all four sides of the inner rectangle.

Double Scalloped Placemat

Next add the scallops to the base placemat. Starting at the corners draw 4" scallops along all 4 sides. Note that the 4" scallops will overlap keeping the Vs of the 3" and 4" scallops lined up.

Trace placemat inset and base onto seperate pieces of freezer paper and cut out.

Making the Base Placemat

Make the placemat with the coffee bean and black fabrics, referring to the Shortcut instructions on page 20.

After trimming the seam allowance and clipping the Vs between the scallops, cut a slit in the coffee bean print and turn right side out through the slit. The center scalloped insert will cover the slit.

Press flat.

Making the Center Scalloped Inset

Thread your machine, both top and bobbin, with water-soluble thread.

Referring to the Shortcut instructions on page 20, make the center scalloped inset using the print and throwaway muslin.

After trimming the seam allowance and clipping the Vs between the scallops, cut a slit in the muslin and turn right side out.

Press the scallops with a hot dry iron to set the seam.

Spray a mist of water on the seam line and press with a steam iron to melt the water-soluble thread.

Gently pull the fabrics apart and discard the throwaway muslin. If the stitches won't let go, repeat the spraying and steaming.

Carefully steam press the entire scalloped inset on both sides.

Remove the water-soluble thread from your machine.

Center the scalloped inset on the placemat, pin in place, and top-stitch in place with matching or invisible thread.

Decorator Towels

Supplies:

- Hand towel
- 4½" x 40" strip of accent fabric (hand towel)
- 3" scallop template
- Bath towel
- 5" x 40" strip of accent fabric (bath towel)
- 4" scallop template
- Water-soluble thread
- Freezer paper

Getting Ready

Measure the width of the towel. Add 1" and trim the strip of accent fabric to that measurement.

Draw a guideline on the wrong side of the accent fabric strip, 1" from the edge for a hand towel or ½" from the edge for a bath towel.

Making the Hand Towel Border Pattern

Draw a rectangle for the hand towel border pattern on freezer paper as shown.

Align the **center point** of the 3" scallop template with the **center** of the lower guideline and draw as many scallops as needed for the width of the pattern.

Repeat along the upper guideline.

Cut out the pattern along the drawn lines.

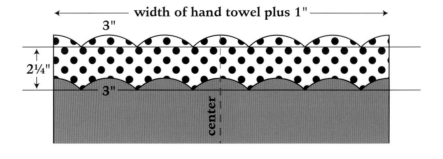

Making the Bath Towel Border Pattern

Draw a rectangle for the bath towel border pattern on freezer paper as shown.

Align the **edge** of the 4" scallop template with the **center** point of the lower guideline and draw as many scallops as needed for the width of the pattern.

Align the **center point** of the 4" scallop template with the **center** of the upper guideline and draw as many 4" scallops as needed for the width of the pattern.

Cut out the pattern along the drawn lines.

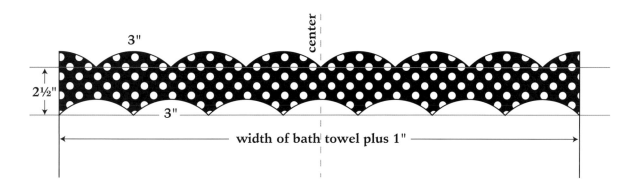

Sewing the Border

Press the freezer-paper pattern to the wrong side of the accent fabric strip, matching the lower guideline of the pattern to the guideline on the fabric.

Trace the scallops onto the fabric. These will be the sewing lines.

Thread your machine, both top and bobbin, with water-soluble thread.

With right sides together, fold the length of the strip in half and pin along the upper scallops.

Stitch the upper scallops along the drawn line.

Trim the seam allowance with pinking shears and trim the points.

Decorator Towels

Turn the strip right side out.

Press the scallops with a hot dry iron to set the seam.

Spray a mist of water on the seam line and press with a steam iron to melt the water-soluble thread.

Gently pull the fabric apart. If the stitches won't let go, repeat the spraying and steaming.

Carefully steam press the turned scallop edge on both sides.

Remove the water-soluble thread from your machine.

Thread the machine to match the accent fabric on top and to match the towel in the bobbin.

Place the accent strip along the back of the towel, aligning the unsewn scallops with the lower edge of the towel, **above any woven edging.**

Stitch along the lower scallops. Trim with pinking shears, clip the Vs between the scallops, turn to the right side, and press.

Turn under the accent fabric seam allowance and pin the scallop strip in place.

Topstitch around the entire scallop strip using matching or invisible thread.

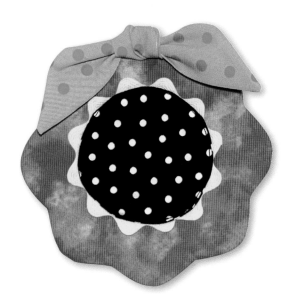

Scalloped Coasters

Supplies:
　½ yard hot pink
　¼ yard or fat quarter black polka dot
　¼ yard or fat quarter green polka dot
　1⅓ yard rickrack or other decorative trim
　Thin cotton batting 13" x 30"
　Freezer paper

Making the Coasters

Cut the batting into four 7" squares and four 4" squares.

Trace the scalloped coaster, coaster center, and coaster bow tie templates onto freezer paper.

Cut out the patterns on the drawn line.

Cut eight 7" squares of hot pink.

On four of the hot pink squares, center and press the scalloped coaster pattern to the wrong side and trace. Remove the pattern.

On a 7" square of batting, place an unmarked 7" square of hot pink right side up and a marked 7" square, marked side up.

Pin in place.

Stitch around coaster on the drawn line. Trim the seam allowance to ¼" with pinking shears and clip the Vs where the scallops meet.

Carefully pull the fabrics apart and clip the center of the marked square. Insert a scissors point and cut a 2" x-shaped opening.

Turn right side out, making sure all the scallops are rounded, and press with a steam iron.

Cut eight 4" squares of black polka dot fabric.

Trace the coaster center pattern onto the back of four squares.

Following the same procedure as for the coasters, layer the marked squares with the unmarked square and the batting. Sew, trim the seam allowance, clip, turn, and press.

Place the center, cut side down, on top of the cut side of the coaster. Tuck the rickrack or decorative trim under the edge of the center and pin in place.

Topstitch the center and decorative trim into place.

Cut and sew four coaster bow ties from the green polka dot fabric as indicated on the template.

Close the opening with hand or machine stitching.

Tie into a single knot to form a bow and tack in place.

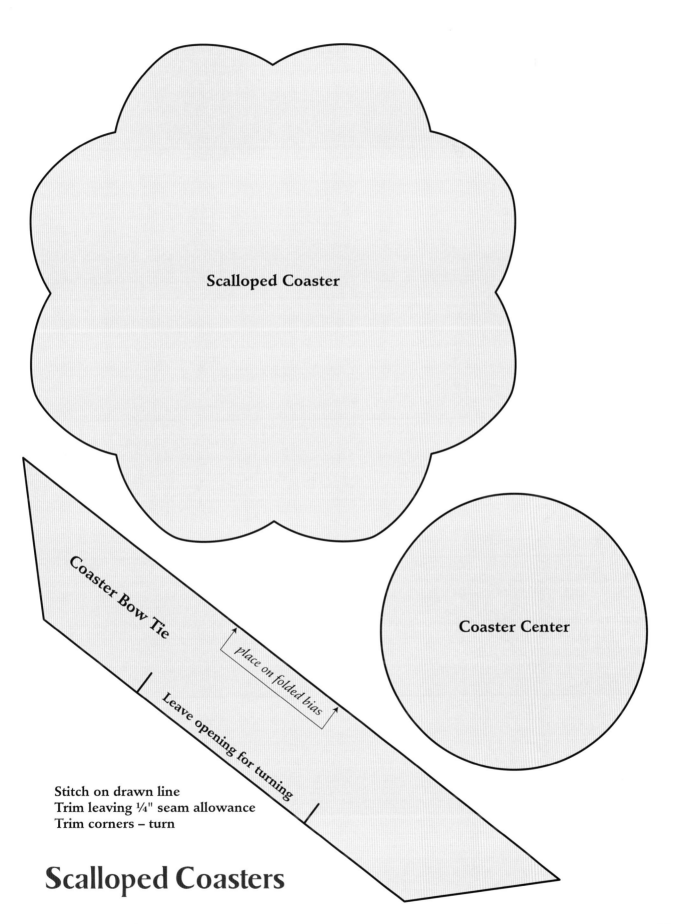

Scalloped Coaster

Coaster Bow Tie

Coaster Center

place on folded bias

Leave opening for turning

Stitch on drawn line
Trim leaving ¼" seam allowance
Trim corners – turn

Scalloped Coasters

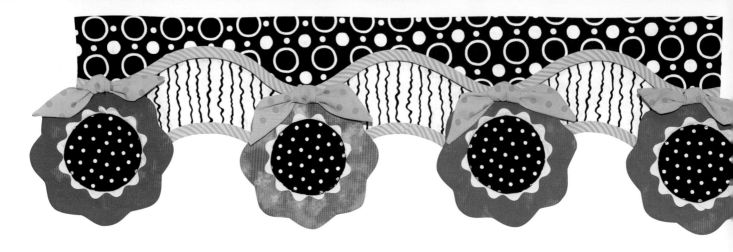

Margaritaville Coaster Dock

Supplies:

3/8 yard black print
3/8 yard striped fabric
2 yards contrasting double-fold bias binding
freezer paper
4" scallop template

Making the Coaster Dock

Cut a piece of freezer paper 11" x 29"

Draw the dock pattern as shown.

Starting in the center of the long side, draw a line of serpentine scallops with the 4" scallop template. Cut out along the drawn line of scallops.

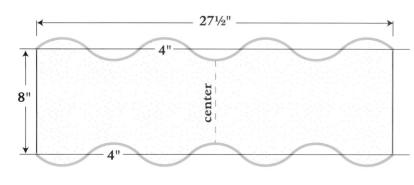

Fold the freezer paper in half, aligning the two long guidelines, and trace the scallops along the second guideline.

Finish cutting out the pattern.

Cut an 11" x 29" rectangle from the print and striped fabric.

Press right sides together and press the freezer-paper pattern to the wrong side of the lighter fabric.

Trace around the pattern and remove the freezer paper.

Cut out the coaster dock and sew along the straight sides only.

Turn right side out and press flat.

Stay stitch around the scallops 1/8" from the edges.

Bind both scalloped edges with the contrasting bias.

Add bits of Velcro® to the scallops and coasters so the coasters can reside on the reef when not in use.

Scalloped Swag Valance

Supplies:
 1 yard striped
 1 yard polka dot
 2¼ yard contrasting bias binding (2½" wide)
 6" scallop template
 Freezer paper

*Yardage given is sufficient for an 18" deep swag with a 3" foldover for a 40" window. For a larger or smaller window, adjust the yardage accordingly.

Making the Valance

Measure the width of the window opening. Determine the depth of the swag and the length of the foldover.

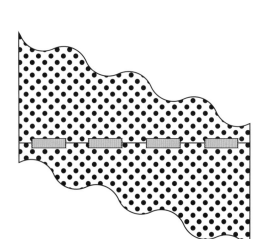

Using these measurements, draw a pattern as shown on a piece of freezer paper cut 2" wider than the depth of the swag and 2" longer than the width of the window opening.

Starting in the center of the longest side, draw shallow serpentine scallops with the 6" scallop template.

Cut out the pattern.

Trace the pattern onto another piece of freezer paper.

Cut out the second pattern and tape it to the first as shown.

Press striped and polka dot fabric with right sides together. Press freezer-paper pattern to the wrong side of lighter fabric.

Cut out around the pattern. Using a ½" seam allowance sew along the straight sides only.

Turn right side out and press flat. Stay stitch around the scallops ⅛" from the edges.

Bind both scalloped edges with the contrasting bias binding.

Fold over a curtain rod and add a rose.

Rose

Supplies:
1 yard tone-on-tone red
1 yard red batik
5" scallop template
freezer paper

Making the Rose

Cut a piece of freezer paper 8" x 48".

Draw a pattern for the rose as shown. Use a ruler with a 45° marking to draw the slanted ends of the pattern.

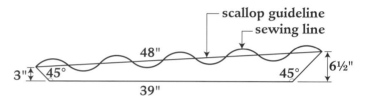

Starting at the wider end of the longest side, draw a serpentine line of 5" scallops.

Cut out the pattern.

Lay the two red fabrics right sides together.

Press the pattern with the scalloped side on the bias as shown.

Trace around the pattern.

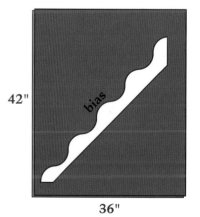

Cut out around the pattern and pin the ends and the scallops.

Sew around three sides; trim the seam allowance with pinking shears, clip the end points, and turn right side out. Press flat.

Sew a running stitch at the raw edges through both layers.

Starting at the narrower end, pull up the running stitch into gathers, rolling the fabric as you go to form the rose. Tack the raw edges together as you roll to hold the petals in place.

Fold the petals outward for a more realistic look.

Descending Scallop Valance

Supplies:

⅞ yard outer fabric
⅞ yard lining fabric
Freezer paper
10" scallop template
7" scallop template

Making the Valance

This valance measurements are for a 40" window. Please make adjustments if your window is a different size.

Cut a piece of freezer paper 28" x 42".

Draw the valance pattern on the freezer paper as shown.

Draw a 10" scallop at the center of the outside guideline.

Draw a 7" scallop at one end of the innermost guideline.

Add an 7" scallop along the middle guideline and a 7" scallop along the outer guideline, overlapping them to fit evenly between the other two scallops. Repeat on the other side.

Cut out the scallops along the drawn line.

Fold the freezer paper in half across the width matching outermost guidelines and trace the scallops.

Cut out entire pattern.

Follow the Turned Edge instructions on pages 20–21 to finish the valance, leave a 6" opening along one of the sides for turning.

Fold over a curtain rod and add a pin or decorative item to the center scallop.

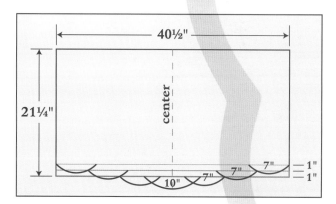

Denim Valance

Supplies:
½ yard denim
½ yard striped fabric
Freezer paper
4" scallop template
3 yards contrasting ribbon

Making the Valance

This valance measurements are for a 40" window. Please make adjustments if your window is a different size.

Cut freezer paper 14" x 42".

Draw the valance pattern on the freezer paper as shown.

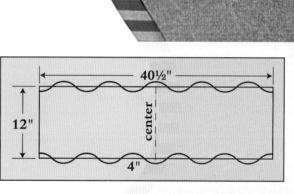

Start in the center of valance. Align the center of the scallop template with the center of the freezer paper pattern and draw a serpentine line of 4" scallops.

Cut out the pattern along the drawn line of scallops.

Fold the freezer paper in half, aligning the two long guidelines, and trace the scallops along the second line.

Finish cutting out the pattern.

Follow the Turned Edge instructions on pages 20–21, leaving a 6" opening along one of the sides for turning.

Fold over curtain rod showing some of the lining. You can reverse the valance for a different look.

Make bows of contrasting ribbon and pin to the scallops.

Denim Pillow

Supplies:
2 pairs of old jeans
4" scallop template

Cutting Instructions

5	6" x 6" squares	Dark denim
4	6" squares	Light denim
4 strips	3½" wide	Make at least 24" long
2	22½" x 13½" rectangles for pillow back

Sewing Instructions

With wrong sides together, sew nine 6" squares into three rows, alternating light and dark denim as illustrated. All seam allowances should be ½" and on the right side of the fabric.

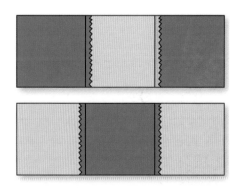

NINE-PATCH BLOCK

With wrong sides together, sew rows together to make a Nine-Patch. Apply coin pockets from jeans to Nine-Patch squares as special embellishments if desired.

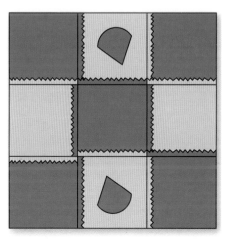

Measure Nine-Patch through the center and cut 2 border strips to that measurement. With wrong sides together, sew onto the sides of the block. Repeat these steps for the top and bottom border.

Clip seam allowances approximately every ½" to make fraying easier.

Denim Pillow

On the right side of the pillow front, draw guidelines 1¼" from the seam line. Using the 4" scallop template, draw scallops starting in the corners on all four sides. Be sure to use removable chalk.

To make an envelope opening for the back of the pillow, hem one long side on each 22½" x 13½" rectangle by folding under and pressing ¼" along one edge. Stitch the hem in place.

Overlap the two hemmed backing pieces to form a 22½" square and pin.

Layer the pillow front and back with wrong sides together. Stitch on the scallop line all around the pillow. Trim the seam allowance to measure ¼". Do not clip this outside seam.

Stitch ⅞" from the 9-patch edge all around the pillow to create the flange. Insert an 18" pillow form.

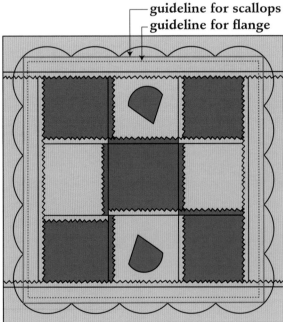

guideline for scallops
guideline for flange

Scallops Sew EASY ✄ *Marie Seroskie*

I Love Paris Pillow

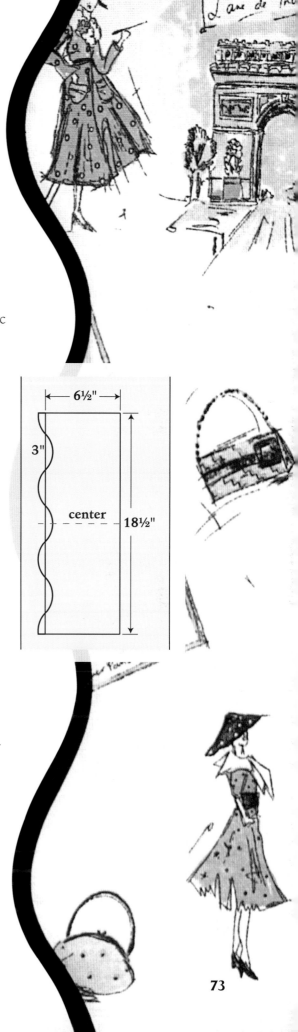

Supplies:

⅝ yard pillow top fabric
¼ yard accent fabric
⅝ yard backing fabric
⅛ yard contrasting fabric
1 yard 1" double-fold bias binding to match the contrasting fabric
Freezer paper
3" scallop template
18" pillow form

Making the Pillow

Cut a piece of freezer paper 9" x 20".

Draw the pillow accent pattern as shown.

Starting in the center of an 18½" side, draw 3" serpentine scallops.

Cut out the pattern.

Cut a 9" x 18½" piece of accent fabric.

Press the pattern to the right side of the accent fabric and trace scalloped edge.

Remove the pattern.

Press folds open on bias tape.

Lay the raw edge of the bias binding along the drawn line of scallops and sew with a ¼" seam allowance.

Trim the accent fabric even with the raw edge of the binding.

Turn the binding to the wrong side of the accent fabric and press in place. The turned-under edge should extend beyond the seam line.

Cut an 18½" square from the pillow top fabric.

Lay the accent on the pillow top as shown.

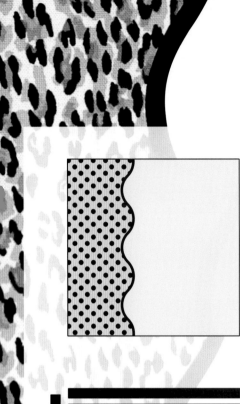

I Love Paris Pillow

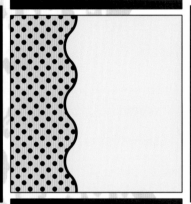

Stitch in the ditch along the bound scalloped edge to secure the binding and accent fabric to the pillow top.

Trim away the excess pillow top fabric from behind the scalloped accent.

Cut two 1" x 40" strips from the contrasting fabric.

Add a border around all four sides of the pillow top using the 1" strips.

To make an envelope opening for the back of the pillow, hem each of the back pieces by folding under and pressing ¼" along one edge and then folding under an additional 6". Stitch the hem in place.

Overlap the two hemmed backing pieces to form a 19½"square, with the hems facing down. Lay the bordered pillow top over the backing pieces, right sides together. Pin in place.

Sew around all four edges with a ¼" seam allowance.

Trim the four corners.

Turn through the envelope opening and press.

Stitch in the ditch along the inside edge of the border to create a narrow flange.

Insert an 18" pillow form.

Scallops Sew EASY *Marie Seroskie*

Scalloped Sheets and Pillow Cases

Supplies:

  Pillow cases and top sheet
  4" scallop template
  Fabric marker
  Thread to match or contrast with sheets *(rayon threads give a beautiful finish)*
  Fine bobbin thread
  Medium to heavy weight stabilizer *(experiment a little to find what works best with your machine)*

Marking the Scallops

Measure the width of the sheet and pillow case to see if 4" scallops will be a good fit and if any adjustments will be necessary.

Draw a guideline 1¼" from the folded edge all around the pillow case opening and along the top cuff of the sheet.

For the pillow cases, mark 5 scallops starting on the folded side of the pillow case, not the seamed side. This will allow for adjustments in the seamed area.

For the top sheet, start marking scallops working from the center out.

Satin Stitching the Scallops

You will need to use two types of stitches in this project, a tiny zigzag and a satin stitch. The zigzag stitch needs to be sewn right on the drawn scallops line. Their purpose is to stabilize the bias edges of the scallops since the scallops need to be cut out before they can be satin stitched.

Thread your machine with the same thread you will use for the satin stitching. Begin with a .05 stitch length and width adjusting as you stitch if necessary. Stitch all of the scallops sewing right on the drawn line.

Using very sharp scissors, trim scallops within a hair of this tiny zigzag.

Set your machine up for a wide satin stitch. Experiment on scrap fabric to get the proper length and width for a beautiful and luxurious satin stitch. Use an open toe foot and place a piece of stabilizer behind your work.

Stitch over the small zigzag stitches you made earlier making sure the needle is just "kissing" the cut side of the fabric. As you stitch down the curve where two scallops meet, continue the stitches a little less than ¼" past the V. Stop with the needle down and then pivot. The needle should be in the outside edge position as it was when you started. If not, you will need to take one more stitch. As you begin satin stitching the next scallop, notice the "diamond" shaped stitches right at the inside where the two satin stitches meet. Check the tension of the bobbin thread as you work.

Some Additional Ideas

Think of adding some decorative stitches following along the scallops or a single embroidery motif. Also don't overlook the idea of serpentine scallops.

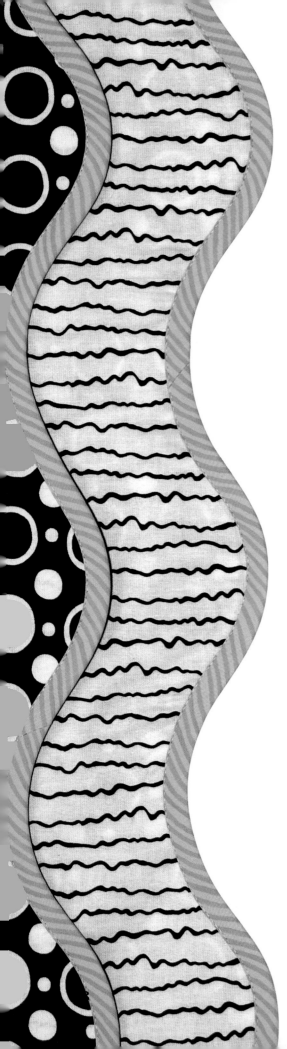

Resources

Katie Lane Quilts
for acrylic scallop templates
www.katielane.com

Superior Threads
www.superiorthreads.com

Fine Machine Sewing Revised Edition:
Easy Ways to Get the Look of Hand Finishing and Embellishing
Carol Laflin Ahles
Newton, Connecticut: The Taunton Press, 2003

Machine Appliqué: A Sampler of Techniques
Sue Nickels
Paducah, Kentucky: American Quilter's Society, 2001

Petal Play the Traditional Way
Joan Shay
Paducah, Kentucky: American Quilter's Society, 2001

Quilter's Complete Guide
Marianne Fons & Liz Porter
Des Moines, Iowa: Oxmoor House, Revised Edition 2001

About
the
Author

arie's interest in quilting began in the late '70s. While tent camping in Vermont with her husband, Jim, she would visit quilt shops and bring back a book or two to the campsite. Finally in the early '80s the quilt bug bit hard. In those days Marie only had the weekends to quilt since she had a demanding full-time job.

In 1986, Marie retired after 30 years in the educational system. Of course, as is typical with new quilters, the first quilts were gifts for others. One quilt, a double bed-sized quilt (lap quilted), is still a reminder of those early quilts.

Marie began teaching quilting in Florida in 1987, at craft and quilt shops. That led to her designing original patterns for classes. As the demand grew to have them available on the commercial market, Katie's Tulip became her first published pattern in 1990. Since then she has published over 40 original patterns. It was also in 1990 that Marie started her own business under the name of Katie Lane Quilts. Katie Lane was the name of the street she and her husband lived on in Orlando, Florida.

Between teaching, lecturing, designing, and publishing patterns as well as a self published book, *Stained Glass Techniques-Art Work in Fabric*, the business kept growing. Jim was the computer guru who not only helped with graphics but was also the editor. Being an engineer, no sentence went unread.

Marie has appeared on *Simply Quilts* with Alex Anderson and on *America Sews* with Sue Hausman. She has written articles that appeared in *Traditional Quiltworks* and *The Professional Quilter*. Katie Lane Quilts Radial Rules have been featured in *Quilter's Newsletter Magazine, Miniature Quilts,* and *Quilting Today*. The original Scallop Radial Rule was featured in the book *Notions... Over 50 Great Gadgets You Can't Live Without* by Taunton Press.

After Marie's husband retired in 2001, they, along with Katie Lane Quilts, moved to Amherst, New Hampshire. People call them the "reverse snowbirds" and Marie finds the seasonal changes and small town life a source of inspiration not only for her patterns, but for the very soul of her being. For the curious, the winter months are just as much appreciated as the other seasons.

other AQS Books

This is only a small selection of the books available from the American Quilter's Society. AQS books are known worldwide for timely topics, clear writing, beautiful color photos, and accurate illustrations and patterns. The following books are available from your local bookseller, quilt shop, or public library.

#7492   us$22.95

#7484   us$22.95

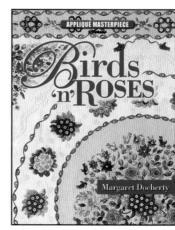

#7013   us$24.95

#7490   us$22.95

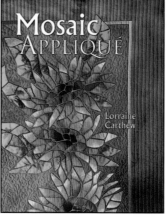

#7071   us$22.95

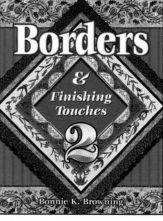

#6804   us$22.95

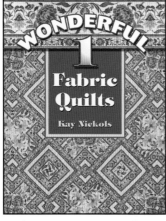

#7487   us$19.95

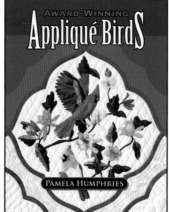

#7494   us$21.95

#7491   us$22.95

Look for these books nationally.
Call or **Visit** our Web site at

1-800-626-5420
www.AmericanQuilter.com